IMAGES
of America

THE SEMINOLE AND MICCOSUKEE TRIBES
OF SOUTHERN FLORIDA

In 1852, the Mikasuki Seminole leader Billy Bowlegs (Potato clan) left the safety of the Florida Everglades to go to Washington, D.C., Boston, and New York City with an "Indian Removal Specialist." The trip was to show the Indians the strength of the United States and the futility of resistance to forced emigration to Indian Territory. Bowlegs's portrait was made September 24, 1852 in Manhattan at the Meade Brothers Broadway Studio. A copy of this photo was taken from Bowlegs's Big Cypress camp when it was invaded November 19, 1857, during the Third Seminole War. (58.)

IMAGES
of America

THE SEMINOLE AND MICCOSUKEE TRIBES OF SOUTHERN FLORIDA

Patsy West

ARCADIA
PUBLISHING

ISBN 978-1-5316-0996-2

Published by Arcadia Publishing
Charleston, South Carolina

Library of Congress Catalog Card Number: 2002108562

For all general information contact Arcadia Publishing at:
Telephone 843-853-2070
Fax 843-853-0044
E-mail sales@arcadiapublishing.com
For customer service and orders:
Toll-Free 1-888-313-2665

Visit us on the Internet at www.arcadiapublishing.com

Creek Seminole Coffee Gopher (Panther clan) poses with young Emma, c. 1906. (71, photograph by E.W. Histed.)

CONTENTS

Charlotte (nee Mary) Tommie shown with her daughter Pricilla Doctor (Snake clan), 1942. (536-9-32, photograph by William D. Boehmer.)

ACKNOWLEDGMENTS

The Seminole/Miccosukee Photographic Archive's collection accumulated from private as well as public sources in a serious retrieval project begun in 1972. It is fortunate that the archive received major photographic contributions over the years, significantly from Henry and Nicole Moretti, Henry and Helen Coppinger, William D. and Edith M. Boehmer, W. Stanley and Mary Ellen Hanson Jr., Alan W. Davis, Dr. John K. Mahon, Dr. James W. Covington, Dr. Charlton W. Tebeau, Dr. Thelma P. Peters, Betty Mae Jumper, Jimmie O. Osceola, Peggy Atzel, and the Washbon family. To others who have shared photographs, data, and identifications I extend a heartfelt thanks: collectors I.S.K. Reeves IV, Katie O. Sweeney, Dennis Lessard, and Tom Moore; museum and archive personnel Susan Gillis, Rebecca Smith, Dawn Hugh, Joan Morris, and Jim Cusik; and to my fellow researchers (the marathoners of microfilm reading) Dr. Joe Knetsch and Dr. Gary Mormino for religiously keeping my own research interests in mind. Finally an extended thanks to the special contributors to this volume: photographers John Gillan, and Robert Kippenberger; Janet Finnegan of *The Creative Source*; Tom Gallaher of the Ah-Tah-Thiki Museum; Virginia Mitchell, editor, and archivist/reporter/photographer Ernie Tiger of Seminole Communications, Seminole Tribe of Florida; and the special assistance of Jimmie O. Osceola and Mary Tiger.

INTRODUCTION

The Seminole/Miccosukee Photographic Archive has been actively engaged in accumulating its collection since 1972. Before that time, the Seminole and Miccosukee tribes had no photograph collections at their disposal. A singular collection of great significance had been systematically accumulated by Dr. William C. Sturtevant, Curator of North American Ethnology at the Smithsonian Institution, as he had conducted his doctoral dissertation on the Florida Indians during the early 1950s. Otherwise, the majority of photos representing these highly identifiable tribal peoples were scattered across the country in public and private, but mostly non-catalogued, collections.

The impetus to organize a comprehensive collection of Seminole/Miccosukee photos arose from my initial position as librarian, and then curator, at the Historical Museum of Southern Florida in Miami. Three large file folders of photographs were labeled "Florida Seminoles," but none of the predominant portraits were identified. Additionally, information on the photographers, who attempted to record the Seminole and Miccosukee with frequent difficulty and hardship, was not available. Their work was dispersed throughout the public and private collections alike, often with little cohesion or provenience available.

My grandmother, Ethel Freeman West, was born in Little River, North Miami, in 1888. The Seminoles were close to her father, William Freeman, and frequented the family yard and boat landing. He hunted with them while a recognized leader, Old Motlow (Wind clan), carried my grandmother around on his shoulders. When the ornithologist Charles Barney Cory, of the Chicago Field Museum, came to the area on one of his many specimen-collecting trips in the early 1890s, he was told to seek out Freeman. My great-grandfather personally introduced him to Robert Osceola (Panther clan) and Cory later credited him with making his tryst with the Seminoles possible. Cory's published work, considered a benchmark in accuracy, was published as *Hunting and Fishing in Florida* and accompanied by his own photographs.

Ironically, the first Seminole family I met as I began my professional career was that of Cory Robert Osceola (Big Towns clan), the son of Robert. Cory Osceola had been named for the scientist that visited them at their camp on the North Fork of New River when he was just a boy. Coincidentally, I have lived on North Fork all my life, only a few miles from the Osceola campsite.

When I began collecting and identifying Seminole photographs, my grandmother was 84 years old. She provided me with the first identifications of Seminoles that were found on glass negatives in the attic of the family house on Little River. Photographs had been taken on that property in 1892 by a Norwegian immigrant, Otto Sonstebo. She told me that my Great Aunt Beck had stood on the back row with the Seminoles to show them they would not be harmed, and ducked out of the way as the shutter was snapped.

My next project was to obtain other identifications. I made identification cards and photocopies of the museum's photographs. I then asked Seminole tribal chairman Howard Tommie if I might set up a table at the Seminole Fair in February. The response at my impromptu booth was great! The late Goby Tiger stands out as an avid resource, as does my longtime friend, Jimmie O'Toole Osceola. Both pondered for many hours over the photograph books at my table, and Jimmie has continued to use the collection ever since.

When the primary photographers' compendium of works and dates was finally organized, the photographs themselves required interpretation. They depicted events, personages, cultural activities, locations, and unique economic endeavors, but most of these had never been discussed in the available popular or scholarly literature. A great deal of data was located in archives or questioned in oral history interviews in order to interpret the photographs. In the case of the tribes' important economic involvement with tourism (depicted in the bulk of the photos), there was the need for primary research and interpretation, which resulted in a serious revision of thought for this important period of economic endeavor. Thus, I began my 30 years of ethnographic studies based on the need to interpret a growing collection of photographs.

The archive's photograph collection now contains well over 10,000 images and dates from 1852 to the present. *Seminole and Miccosukee Tribes of Southern Florida* will provide tribal members and other readers with an organized visual and historical resource. Though brief, it will nevertheless serve as a valuable introduction to the unique culture of two sovereign tribal nations that continue to flourish in southern Florida today.

Author's Note: There are two distinct, unintelligible languages spoken by Florida Indians: Mikasuki (*i:laponathli:*), and Creek (or *Muscogee*). These distinctions of language divide the two groups of culturally similar people. Approximately two-thirds of the total population (regardless of tribal membership) reflect a Mikasuki linguistic background; the remaining third, Creek.

There are, as the book title suggests, two distinct tribes in southern Florida: the Seminole Tribe of Florida, federally recognized in 1957, and the Miccosukee Tribe of Indians of Florida, federally recognized in 1961.

Seminole tribal members include those people of Creek linguistic heritage (centered at Brighton Reservation and Ft. Pierce). Approximately two-thirds of Seminole tribal members are people of Mikasuki linguistic heritage who reside on the other four Seminole reservations: Tampa, Immokalee, Big Cypress, and Hollywood. The Miccosukee Tribe consists exclusively of those people with a Mikasuki linguistic heritage. They reside along the Tamiami Trail, and they have the virtually unpopulated Miccosukee Reservation and other property in Big Cypress at their disposal.

Before the 1950s, all Indians in southern Florida were called "Seminole." For the sake of clarity, I will use the designation "Seminole" for photographs taken before 1950. It should be understood that unless subjects are specifically designated as "Creek Seminole," they are of the Mikasuki heritage. Select photos after 1950 will continue to use the linguistic "Creek Seminole" designation, but "Seminole" and "Miccosukee" after this date will also refer to tribal affiliation. Those identified as "Independent" are those Mikasuki-speaking families who chose not to affiliate with either federally designated tribe.

One

THE FLORIDA SEMINOLES AND MICCOSUKEES

Following two major 19th century wars of removal during which some 6,000 Florida Indians surrendered or were captured and shipped to the Oklahoma Territory, the 200 Seminole survivors reorganized and resumed their trading economy in furs, bird plumes, and alligator hides. Robert Osceola (Panther clan) and Doctor Tiger's Boy (Wind clan) pay a visit to the Jupiter Lighthouse at Jupiter, Florida in 1879. This rare stereopticon card is of a photograph by Melville Spencer. (92.17.1.)

13440 LAKE WORTH AND THE ROYAL POINCIANA, PALM BEACH, FLA.

Tourism was made possible by the arrival of Henry Flagler's Florida East Coast Railroad in the latter 1890s. The "Seminoles," as all of the Florida Indians were then called, emerged as a bonus. A postcard from the Detroit Publishing Co. shows an unidentified Seminole posing by a coconut tree. Across Lake Worth is Flagler's exclusive Royal Poinciana Hotel at Palm Beach. (1788.)

Tallahassee (Deer clan) poses with accessories once typical for elite Seminole men in a photograph c. 1900 by Frederick Andrew Metcalfe. The sashes are of two distinct types: one is embroidered beadwork on wool, while the other is heddle-loomed woolen yarn with large beads added during the weaving process. The latter technique was used for the garters, while the leggings exhibit beadwork embroidery on wool. (442.)

Moff-ci-huf-tie, Lucy Fewell (Mrs. Cufney Tiger) (Panther clan), poses near her mother's banana patch, *c.* 1905. Around her neck are strands of necklace beads topped with necklaces made of pierced coins. On the bodice-ruffle are four beaten silver bangles (three made from a silver dollar and one from a quarter); she also wears a gingham skirt with two ruffles. (109.)

These Bird clan women, heavily laden with beads, coin necklaces, and silver bangles, have been identified as Ben Well's mother and Suzie Tiger. They were Creek Seminoles who lived near Lake Okeechobee. The men are unidentified. (91.5P.18, William D. and Edith M. Boehmer Collection.)

11

On the Miami River, Little Charlie Jumper (Panther clan) and Billie Tommie Jumper (Bear clan) pose with their children in a cypress dugout canoe, laden with camp gear, c. 1904. (1020.)

The gregarious Creek Seminole, Captain Tom Tiger (Wildcat clan), lived with his two Mikasuki Snake clan wives near Lake Okeechobee. He met the first train to the area and later greeted President Arthur. Tiger's bones were later stolen by a speculator in 1907, nearly causing hostilities until they were returned. His photograph was made into postcards by several studios from Palatka to Miami. (1148.)

Mikasuki women *Nittarkee, Otta hee* (Panther clan), and *Follee Tikee* (Bird clan) pose in a Miami photographic studio, *c.* 1904. Charlie Tiger (Bird clan) and Charlie Billie (Wildcat clan) stand with trading post operator James Girtman. (782.)

A Family of Indians from the Everglades, near Miami, Fla
JULIUS SMITH, MIAMI, FLA.

An unidentified family poses in perhaps the same Miami studio, *c.* 1904. This photograph was made into a postcard by Julius Smith. (498.)

A stuffed alligator was a popular photographic studio prop that was associated with the Miami photographer Fred Hand's studio. Seminole children were frequently referred to as "papoose" or "pickaninny" around 1900. (1125, postcard published by J.N. Chamberlain.)

A postcard, doubtless made from a photograph by Hand in Miami c. 1900, was of Old Charlie Osceola (Panther clan) who resided on New River in Ft. Lauderdale. Charlie remembered as a young boy seeing family members rounded up to be sent off to Indian Territory. (20.)

Billy Bowlegs III (Little Black Snake clan) was of no relation to the war leader. This Bowlegs was a grandchild of one of the last full-blood African slaves owned by a Seminole clan. His mother Nancy was half-Seminole, a slave retained by the Snake Clan. Since Seminole mothers give their clan to their children and Billy's mother had no clan, he was given the designation of Little Black Snake clan by his Seminole relatives, c. 1911. (1322.)

Ruby Tiger Tail (Wind clan) grew up in one of the earliest families of Seminole entrepreneurs in trade and tourism. Ruby exhibits her own affluence with an abundance of beads and silver bangles. She holds her arm across her mid-drift in a characteristic pose affected by Seminole women of this era, before the ruffles on their bodice were modestly lengthened to form a cape, c. 1915. (316.) (Photograph by Julian A. Dimock.)

Both the Snake Clan and the Bird Clan have narratives of young women escaping from the U.S. military en route to Indian Territory during the Seminole Wars. During the Third Seminole War (1855–1858), *Ma-de-lo-yee*, Polly Parker, (Little Bird clan), and others escaped when the steamship they were on stopped to take on wood in north Florida. Relocated with relatives, Polly Parker's saga made her a legend in her own time. (424, photograph by H.E. Hill)

Two

THE RESIDENCES OF
THE CLANS

Home of the Seminoles, Pine Island, Fla.

The post-war settlements were large, with ceremonial grounds nearby, and were located near Lake Okeechobee in the Big Cypress and at Pine Island in the eastern Everglades. The three islands of the Pine Island complex were occupied by the Seminoles before the second Seminole War in 1835. In 1897, when this photograph was taken, there were two camps on Pine Island alone. (449, photograph by H.A. Ernst; postcard by Hugh C. Leighton Co., Portland, Maine.)

Mary (Mrs. Smallpox) Tommie's (Bird clan) camp in the lower Everglades was photographed from the Good Year Blimp *Defender* while on a promotional flight during an Opa Locka air show in July of 1929. Mrs. Tommie later recalled that as this blimp flew over, she was very frightened and hid in her banana patch until dark. Notice the canoe channels and docks, the central cooking *chickee*, and the hog pen on the right. (188-30, photograph by Claude C. Matlack. Courtesy of the Historical Museum, Miami.)

In this matrilineal society, the eldest woman was the head of her camp. Children were born into their mother's clan, and all clan members were considered relatives. Marriage was to a member of another clan; therefore, the husbands who came to her camp to live were the only outsiders. Sally Cypress (Panther clan) poses by the campfire at her camp with her niece Marion, *c.* 1920. (88.5.1433, W. Stanley Hanson Sr. Collection.)

This low island in the Big Cypress is seen during a season of high water—a good reason why the Seminoles' house, the *chickee*, had its living quarters built off the ground. Once the Seminoles could purchase used Model-T Fords and trucks, canoes became obsolete, and families were sometimes stranded on islands until the water went down, *c.* 1930s. (88.5.1843, W. Stanley Hanson Sr. Collection.)

This Creek Seminole camp in a cabbage palm hammock shows why the Creeks living around Lake Okeechobee were sometimes called the "Cabbage Palm" group, *c.* 1925. (96.15.6, Rev. Alexander Linn Collection.)

This is a Creek Seminole camp in a cabbage palm hammock *c.* 1940s. Looking down the driveway, the Creeks, living on higher ground, kept horses along with their cars. (91.5P.19, photograph by William D. Boehmer.)

Building a *chickee* required the help of several people. The upright posts in the Creek environs were frequently made of cabbage palm (seen here), while the Mikasukis used cypress trees. The most time-consuming task was cutting and transporting the palmetto "fans," to which the Creeks on the Okeechobee prairies had easier access. (429–3, photograph by William D. Boehmer.)

There was a task for everyone in the operation of the Seminole camp. Here Ben Wells, an elderly man, tacks a nail in the fan. The next step is to hand the fan to a man on the roof, who will then twist and nail it into place on a beam of the framework, c. 1960. (429–2, photograph by William D. Boehmer.)

A *chickee* is shown under construction, on Brighton Reservation in July 1961. A man hands a fan to the worker on the roof. The quality and longevity of a *chickee* depends on how close the stems of the fans are nailed together. (61–4, photograph by William D. Boehmer.)

On the *chickee* platform above the damp ground, it was dry. Clothes, bedding, and mosquito nets were rolled up under the eaves in the daytime. Small containers of valuables and sewing notions were tucked away on rafters from which the baby's rope cradle was suspended. The baby probably took its first steps on the *chickee* platform supervised by Minnie Micco (Otter clan). (88.5.1868, photograph by W. Stanley Hanson Sr. Collection.)

The Seminoles, especially the Mikasuki speakers living in the Everglades and Big Cypress, traveled frequently. Some clans maintained two permanent settlements, one in the Big Cypress and the other on the eastern coastal ridge with access to the rivers and ocean, *c.* 1910. (411.)

When a camp moved, utensils and animals were packed and the occupants lived in tents made of tarpaulins. The family of *Arteyee* Tiger Osceola (Bird clan) and her husband John Osceola (Big Towns clan) with children Lena, Eva, Mary, and Bennett pose in a temporary camp on New River at Ft. Lauderdale, *c.* 1925. (1701.)

Ruby Cypress (Panther clan) cooks while her husband Whitney (Otter clan) puts kindling on the fire in the cooking *chickee* at her Big Cypress camp *c.* 1925. Seminole fires are unique, as the placement of the logs enables a single fire, properly tended, to last for weeks. (96.15.2, Rev. Alexander Linn Collection.)

Billy Bowlegs III (Little Black Snake clan) tends his fire with a small palmetto fan while seated in his camp on the Brighton Reservation, c. 1940s. Most cooking *chickees* contained shelving for cans of foodstuffs, salt, lard, and coffee, safely sealed away from the south Florida humidity and pests. A work area table built in the shade of a tree. (91.5P.20, photograph by William D. Boehmer.)

In this "real photo" postcard, *Mokee* Tiger (Mrs. Doctor Tiger) (Wind clan) is seen in a temporary camp. Her canoe is in the foreground. Under the palmetto fans on the left is probably a cache of coontie roots that she will later process into starch. (703.)

From the amount of felled lumber and older debris in the area, it is probable that this temporary campsite was at a location frequented by groups of Seminole woodcutters. It appears that they were engaged in dressing posts (see left) for a new *chickee*. (88.5.1775, W. Stanley Hanson Sr. Collection.)

Often the Seminoles made more permanent platforms, such as this one, in trading areas that they would frequent several times during a year. All they had to do when they arrived was to throw a tarp over the ridgepole and make themselves at home. Note the thickness of the split logs. (88.5.1498, W. Stanley Hanson Sr. Collection.)

Three

GETTING AROUND IN SOUTH FLORIDA

Robert Osceola (Panther clan) steers his canoe after a manatee on New River. Manatee meat, which is similar in taste to pork, was a common food to the Seminole families that frequented the coastal areas of the lower Florida peninsula. This photograph was taken from another boat by Charles Barney Cory, c. 1895. (15.)

Seminole canoes were generally fitted with a step to hold a sailing mast. When they left the wide Miami River and entered the narrow south fork, canoeists stowed their sails and employed the push pole for steerage. Masts were left erect so that they could raise sail once they entered the open area of the Everglades, c. 1904. (989, photograph by J.N. Chamberlain.)

W.S. Blatchley was on the Kissimmee River March 1, 1913, and wrote of this photograph: "Saw a sail coming through the bushes. On rounding the bend, found it to be a dugout cypress canoe." In the canoe was a young Seminole man, "two hound dogs and a bundle or two of furs. The wind was from the south and made his sailing easy. I Kodaked him..." (960.)

Children, both boys and girls, learned the art of canoeing by trial and error. Here two boys try to pole a large canoe with a girl passenger through grasses. This postcard was published by the Hugh C. Leighton Co. of Portland, Maine, c. 1904. (727.)

SEMINOLE INDIAN FAMILY IN DUG-OUT CANOE
ON MIAMI RIVER, FLORIDA.

With large canoes such as this one, an entire family, household goods, and livestock could be moved. This particular canoe is approximately 30 feet long. The photograph was taken c. 1915, and the postcard was published by the H. & W.B. Drew Co., Jacksonville, Florida. (02.2.1.)

Charlie Tiger (Bird clan) poles his smaller hunting or work canoe through a Big Cypress waterway. His ax rests on the bow platform, *c.* 1930s. (96.3.7.)

In times of extreme drought, the Seminoles sometimes had to move their canoes to water with ox carts or wagons. Travel was especially critical in late May or early June, when families needed to journey to the annual Green Corn Dance. Here a Creek family near Ft. Pierce moves their canoes to water, *c.* 1904. (1012, photograph by H.E. Hill; postcard published by the Cochrane Co., Palatka, Florida.)

SEMINOLE INDIAN.
HUNTING IN THE EVERGLADES, FLORIDA.

A young woman poles her canoe in the Big Cypress with her toddler inside. The distal end of the push pole had a unique "boot" attached. This allowed the canoeist to push off the oolitic limestone bottom without getting the pole stuck in the overlying mud, *c.* 1930s. (88.5.1645, W. Stanley Hanson Sr. Collection.)

A photograph of Seminoles canoeing on the Miami River around 1902 was taken by J.N. Chamberlain. Seen in popular publications, it was also published as a postcard. (1789.)

More than a dozen Seminole dugouts were rafted together on the bank of the Miami River, one block north of the Flagler Bridge in front of Captain Mann's home. Billy Buck stands in the bow of one with his rifle. Mann's Landing was the popular place for the Seminoles to raft their canoes and camp while trading in Miami, July 28, 1911. (490, photograph by Jesse H. Bratley.)

Canoes are beached at a camp on Chokoloskee Island, near the southwestern tip of Florida, c. 1913. Families living in the Big Cypress, such as the Futch (Otter clan) and Ruby (Panther) Cypresses, would sometimes leave from Chokoloskee and head east to Miami, traveling around the tip of Florida at night when the waves were calm rather than going through the Everglades. (961, photograph by John K. Small.)

Big Cypress resident Charlie Cypress (Otter clan), brother of Futch, was a renowned canoe builder all of his life. Here he shapes the canoe's bottom with an ax. (91.5P.30, William D. and Edith M. Boehmer Collection.)

Creek Seminoles on horseback and in ox carts journey to the Green Corn Dance in the late spring, 1890s. (1003, photograph by Charles Barney Cory.)

Wilson Cypress (Otter clan) is shown with one of his oxen in his wife Ruby Cypress's Panther camp *Californee*, c. 1925. Wilson was a successful hunter who depended on his oxen to transport his furs and alligator hides to market. His caches of hides were often mentioned in the Ft. Myers newspapers. (96.15.1, Rev. Alexander Linn Collection.)

Creeks from the Okeechobee area visited the Stranahan Trading Post on New River in Ft. Lauderdale in the late 1890s. From left to right are Mrs. Jim Gopher (Wildcat clan), Mrs. Billy Stewart (Bird clan), and Lake Wilson (Bird clan), standing beside Robert Osceola's wagon and white horse. (118, photograph by Katherine E. McClellan. Courtesy of Ft. Lauderdale Historical Society.)

Eventually, the canoe and the ox cart were replaced by the flivver. Even in the Big Cypress, a flivver (except in abnormally high water) could easily be driven. If it bogged down in mud holes, it was jacked up with the aid of a sapling and some strong arms, and the journey continued. Shown from left to right are Homespun Billie (Otter clan), Wilson Doctor (Big Towns clan), and Frank Tucker (Otter clan). (1698.)

Four

PEOPLE HELD TOGETHER BY CULTURAL TRADITIONS

Life began in a small, thatched shelter that was built outside the camp specifically for women in labor. A death in the confines of a camp dictated that the camp would be abandoned. Thus, should the mother die in childbirth, the shelter afforded protection to the camp. This is another "real photo" postcard. (699.)

A postcard illustrates a Seminole woman carrying a baby on her back. Until children could walk, they rode in a sling on the back of their female relatives. (02.3.1, photograph by J.N. Chamberlain.)

Creek Seminole Fred Smith (Bird clan) exhibits the traditional tonsured, first-haircut for a boy. (91.5P.21, photograph by William D. Boehmer.)

Children pose in the Big Cypress Panther clan camp of Little Nancy and Little Billie, August 1910. Children were expected to engage in the operation of the camp as soon as they were old enough to carry water. Giving a guest a drink was often their first official task. (476, photograph by Julian A. Dimmock.)

Children were with their mother or female relatives at all times. Here Mary Cypress (Wind clan) washes clothes in the Big Cypress with Buck and Stanley Hanson, c. 1929. (88.5.1698, W. Stanley Hanson Collection.)

The Green Corn Dance was the Seminoles' most important annual socio-religious event. Seldom attended by outsiders and never photographed, it was where children received names, marital status was noted, and criminals were punished. This dance was held at Rock Island in 1938. Ceremonial, social dances were a highlight of the four-day event. Here, on the forth day, Charlie Cypress (Otter clan) leads a line of dancers. (1989–011–8672, photograph by Charles Ebbets; Courtesy of the Historical Museum, Miami.)

The Seminoles' medicine bundle carrier, or his assistant, made *scarifiers* (scratchers) out of turkey quills (here shown by Josie Billie, Panther clan) handily bent into rectangles and studded on one side with four needles. (478, photograph by William D. Boehmer.)

Scratching with a turkey quill *scarifier* was for ceremonial purification at the Corn Dance. Men would be scratched on the arms, legs, back, and chest. Scratching/bloodletting for children and adults was culturally practiced for both therapeutic and disciplinary reasons in order to get bad blood out. (480–4, photograph by William D. Boehmer.)

Josie Billie (Panther clan) was one of the most influential medicine men and holders of medicine bundles until his death in the late 1970s. Here he discusses the importance of the four directions in Seminole life. (83–125–266, photograph by Russell Peithman; Courtesy of Florida State Archives)

Creek Seminole Emma Micco (Bird clan) and Henley Josh (Bird clan) pound corn into meal with pestles. Corn meal, with which corn sofki was made, was a staple of the Seminole diet, c. 1950s. (473–4, photograph by William D. Boehmer.)

Creek Seminole Mary Osceola Huff (Bird clan) is engaged in the process of sifting corn meal into a palmetto splint basket at the Brighton Reservation. She rests on a typical camp work platform, c. 1960s. (518–56, photograph by William D. Boehmer.)

Creek Seminole Emma Micco (Bird clan) is seen making a palmetto splint-sifting basket that was used to separate the chaff from the useable corn meal, c. 1948. (91.5P.22, photograph by William D. Boehmer.)

Mary Motlow Osceola (Bird clan) makes *lapali*, large flat pan bread cooked in a skillet, at the Florida Folk Festival at White Springs, in March 1964. (91.5P.23, photograph by William D. Boehmer.)

Creek Seminole Mary Osceola Huff (Bird clan) holds pans of *lapali*. She wears a hairstyle frequently adopted by Creek Seminole matrons, *c.* 1960. (433–1, photograph by William D. Boehmer.)

Whitney Cypress (Otter clan) makes a *sofki* spoon, using a stump of a cabbage palmetto tree as a work-table, on the Big Cypress Reservation, *c.* 1950s. (91.5P.24, photograph by William D. Boehmer.)

Creek Seminole Billy Smith (Panther clan), holder of the important Creek medicine bundle, poses in his spring corn garden. His garden was in a rich hammock that had been cleared by girdling or cutting around the trunks of trees, a typical Seminole agricultural practice, 1911. (425–25, photograph by Lorenzo D. Creel; William D. and Edith M. Boehmer Collection.)

The Pine Island complex was abandoned around 1900 due to the encroachment of settlers. The residents dispersed into small, isolated camps on islands in the south and western Everglades. Their crops were often planted some distance away and the garden was infrequently tended. Pumpkin vines grew up the cornstalks and covered the garden plot to keep in moisture and choke out weeds, c. 1910. (955, photograph by Julian A. Dimmock.)

Dr. Tiger (Panther clan) presses cane with a commercial press near his sugarcane field in the Big Cypress. The juice would later be boiled for syrup and sugar, c. 1930s. (46.)

On the Brighton Reservation, Creek Seminoles Mary Huff and Mahala and Leona Smith (Bird clan) cut up hearts of palm to make "Swamp cabbage," which will be boiled with pork rind, while Leoma Smith looks on. Palm hearts, a gourmet delicacy in city markets, were commercially cut at the Brighton Reservation and sold to canneries. (79.1.1, photograph by Henry Moretti.)

Creek Seminole Alice Micco (Bird clan) fishes at the Brighton Reservation on Harney Pond Canal, c. 1942. (3–19, photograph by William D. Boehmer.)

Wilson Cypress (Otter clan) and a grandson fish with a gig in their Big Cypress camp, 1940. (733.)

Five

LIVING AND PROSPERING
OFF THE LAND

Around 1880 these men posed for the camera on Florida's west coast. Seen in the front row from left to right are Johnny Osceola (Panther clan), Water Turkey (Bear clan), Henry Clay (Otter clan), and Charlie Billie (Panther clan). The bows and arrows were used to hunt small game and fish. Pictured from left to right in the back row are Billy Motlow (Panther clan), Billy Fewell (Wind clan), Francis A. Hendry, Jimmie Osceola (Panther clan), and Charlie Dixie, whose African-American mother was a slave of the Bird clan. (3.)

The Stranahan Trading Post on New River in Ft. Lauderdale was the focal point of trade for Seminoles of the Pine Island complex. Begun in 1893, Frank Stranahan catered to the Seminoles' needs, adding a shelter for overnight stays (in background) and a boatslip off the river. Furs, bird plumes, and alligator hides were traded to obtain salt for tanning and flour for bread. (129, Courtesy of Ft. Lauderdale Historical Society.)

Seminole men, more than Seminole women, were anxious to add clothing accessories to their native attire. This postcard, c. 1904, shows the family of Mrs. Charlie Willie (Bird clan) in Miami. From the traders Brickell or Girtman Bros., they had purchased bowlers, a straw hat, vests, watch fobs, shoes, neckties, trousers, dress shirts, and a coat, while the women solely retained their traditional attire. (1218.)

William Brickell's Trading Post was built in the 1870s on Biscayne Bay at the mouth of the Miami River, a major Everglades artery. (1595, Courtesy of the Historical Museum, Miami.)

Corn Billie (Panther clan) and John Osceola (Big Towns) are engaged in an alligator hunt up the Miami River in this "real photo" postcard, c. 1929. Corn has pushed a steel brake rod from a Model-T Ford down into the gator's den under the riverbank. He holds the metal rod in his teeth and grunts like an alligator. When the sound reverberates down into the den, the alligator will swim out to see who is invading his territory, and John Osceola will shoot it. (642.)

An atypical business was Charlie Tiger Tail's Store, located in the lower Everglades at the head of Rock Creek. Charlie (Wind clan) was a literate businessman who purchased his fellow Seminoles' hides and furs and sold them to the market directly, 1910. (1195, photograph by Julian A. Dimmock.)

Tom Osceola (Panther clan) is seen on a hunt with his double barrel shotgun. He has his burden strap (which will hold the haunch of deer if he is successful), ammunition bag, and knives, c. 1913. (88.5.1586, W. Stanley Hanson Sr. Collection.)

Charlie Willie's Store was located on an island in the lower Everglades. Like Tiger Tail, Willie (Big Towns clan) purchased from the Seminoles and sold to the market. Willie was married to Sally Willie (Bird clan). The Willies had left Pine Island around 1900 and moved into the southwestern Everglades, c. 1917. (936, photograph by Henry Coppinger Jr.)

Ted Smallwood's store, located on an island on Chokoloskee Bay near the extreme southwestern tip of Florida, is shown in this postcard. The store was built on pilings due to flooding from seasonal tides and hurricanes. Elderly Seminoles, who camped on the property as youths, remember that they could leave items under the store and come back days later to retrieve them. (582.)

Abraham Lincoln Clay (Panther clan) holds a small alligator that he has just shot, *c.* 1920. (1005.)

A Creek Seminole woman is seen here preparing a raccoon skin for drying, *c.* 1940. (536–9–14, photograph by William D. Boehmer.)

Six

TOURISM DOLLARS FOR BEING THEMSELVES

The drainage of the eastern Everglades was made possible by a series of canals dredged from Lake Okeechobee south to East Coast rivers. The New and Miami Rivers were the southern termini of this massive reclamation project. In a poignant photograph taken March 27, 1920, Miami photographer Claude C. Matlack questioned the plight of the Seminoles. (5–30, Courtesy of the Historical Museum, Miami.)

Tony Tommie poses for a publicity shot with a starlet from *Idol Dancer* by D.W. Griffith, one of the earliest movies filmed in Ft. Lauderdale, against the backdrop of the pristine New River. For the movie, Seminoles played Polynesian dancers. (5–3485, Courtesy of Ft. Lauderdale Historical Society.)

The popular tourist attractions featuring Seminole Indians began when Miami tour companies realized that Northern tourists enjoyed seeing the natives in their colorful striped patchwork clothing. Buses visited temporary camps of Mikasuki-speaking Seminoles such as this one, but business was tenuous since they did not stay long, c. 1917. (164, photograph by Henry Coppinger Jr.)

Tourists visited Annie Jumper Tommie's Panther clan camp at the north fork of New River at Broward Boulevard, c. 1919. Pictured from left to right are as follows: (front row) Frank Huff, Alice Huff, Lena Huff, and Pocahontas Huff; (back row) Eulah Mae Fewell, unidentified, Willie Jumper, unidentified, and Annie Jumper Tommie, c. 1919. (149.)

Henry Coppinger Sr. owned a tropical garden on the south fork of the Miami River. A tour company asked if he would include a Seminole Indian village as a feature of his business. The first family he hired was that of Mrs. Jack Tiger Tail (Big Towns clan). Jack Tiger Tail (Wind clan) was very popular in Miami. Shown here in 1921, he poses in the studio of R.W. Harrison for an important publicity shot. (166, Henry Coppinger Jr. Collection.)

Developed on drained Everglade land northwest of Miami by cattleman James Bright and airplane pioneer Glenn Curtiss, the new town of Hialeah (meaning "High Prairie" in the Mikasuki language) opened in March 1921 with a Seminole theme. Shown here are the 20–32 foot billboards of Jack Tiger Tail, which point the way from the state line south, 1921. (x340, photograph by William A. Fishbaugh; Courtesy of Florida State Archives, Tallahassee.)

In a 1922 publicity shot, a Hialeah bus with Seminole passengers advertises Willie Willie's Alligator Farm and Musa Isle Grove, outside the Curtiss-Bright Ranch Office in Hialeah. Willie Willie (Bird clan) had a Seminole village at Musa Isle Grove, but he mysteriously lost his concession. (420, photograph by William A. Fishbaugh; Courtesy Florida State Archives, Tallahassee.)

Musa Isle Seminole Village was on the Miami River. Two cooking *chickees* were built since different clans did not cook together. The alligator wrestling-pit faced the river. There was also a zoo and a trading post that sold a variety of goods including Seminole crafts, *c.* 1937. (221, photograph by WPA photographer, Florence I. Randle; Florence I. Randle Collection.)

The Seminole village at Coppinger's, later renamed Pirate's Cove, was nestled in the lush setting of a tropical garden with lofty Royal Palms. (169, Henry Coppinger Jr. Collection.)

Since both Seminole Villages, Coppinger's Pirate's Cove and Musa Isle, were on the Miami River, their main venue for tourists, besides tour buses, was the sightseeing boat. The *Dixie* delivered to Coppinger's and the *Seminole Queen* to Musa Isle. Both berthed at the downtown Miami Pier, March 12, 1942. (97.3.16.)

The exciting sport of alligator wrestling was most popular with the tourists. While Seminole men dealt with alligators in the wild, alligator wrestling as a show-stopping attraction feature was perfected by Henry Coppinger Jr. and copied by young Seminole men. Here tourists watch alligator wrestling at Musa Isle. (751, Tommy Carter Collection.)

Henry "Cowboy" Billie (Big Towns clan) bulldogs the gator and performs a dangerous trick in this "real photo" postcard. Putting his head between the alligator's jaws, the flourish is in letting go of the jaws for the final seconds. Sure to bring gasps from the audience, the wrestler receives great applause and tips. (1664.)

These young women grew up at Musa Isle. Seen in this "real photo" postcard are, from left to right, Mittie Osceola Jim, Annie Doctor Jimmie, Lena Osceola Billie (Big Towns clan), Annie Billie, Mickey Tiger, and Maggie Billie Buster (others are Bird clan). They were photographed by WPA photographer Florence I. Randle, c. 1937. (76.)

The Seminole families of the tourist attractions carried on their daily routine and stayed at the attractions only as long as they desired. This photograph shows Bird clan employees of the Musa Isle tourist attraction preparing a meal of garfish. From left to right are unidentified, Mickey Tiger, unidentified, and Mrs. John Tiger, c. 1937. (243, photograph by WPA photographer Florence I. Randle; Florence I. Randle Collection.)

When Willie Willie (Bird clan) left Musa Isle, the Hialeah promoters set him up in their "Sport Section." His large village might have been a great success, but it was instead obliterated in the disastrous 1926 hurricane. He then retired in ill health to Dania Reservation. (75g, photograph by Gleason Waite Romer. Courtesy of the Miami-Dade County Public Library System, Romer Collection.)

The Seminole Indian Village at the Canadian National Exhibition in Toronto, August 1931, featured Seminoles from Miami managed by Henry Coppinger Jr. All of the palmetto fans had been packed in boxcars and shipped for the entranceway and village *chickees*, with coconut trees brought for landscaping. (739.)

The popularity of the commercial Seminole Indian Villages was so great that a village opened upstate at Silver Springs and was later named "Ross Allen's Seminole Indian Village." Lee (Panther clan) and Charlie (Otter clan) Cypress (seated on the left) took their family from the Big Cypress to populate this attraction for many seasons, February 12, 1939. (412, photograph by the Burgert Brothers Studio, Tampa.)

At the end of the short "tourist season," the Seminoles from Musa Isle Tourist Attraction were delivered back to their camps along the Tamiami Trail in a large truck. Head-man of the Seminole village, Cory Osceola (Big Towns clan) stands with owner (Egbert L.) Bert Lasher, and Mary, Mrs. Jimmie Druitt Osceola's family (Bird clan), in this "real photo" postcard. Cory Osceola became the spokesman for the non-reservation Seminoles, c. 1930. (00.53.1, Mary Osceola Moore Collection.)

A close associate of the Big Cypress Seminoles, W. Stanley Hanson Sr. organized some 70 people for a special engagement at the Bok Singing Tower, an old Florida attraction, in Lake Wales, Florida, March 1937. These *i:laponi:* (Mikasuki-speakers) represented nearly one-fifth of their population in an economy that they created and monopolized. (88.5.7, W. Stanley Hanson Sr. Collection.)

SEMINOLES! The Only American Indians Whom Your Uncle Sam Never Conquered or Ruled.

A rotogravure photograph was published February 26, 1937 to advertise the Florida Indians' unconquered status, which was a significant tourist asset. The photograph, taken a decade earlier by Claude C. Matlack at Miami's premier Musa Isle Seminole Indian Village tourist attraction, features head-man Tony Tommie (Panther clan) standing with attraction owner Bert Lasher. (1297.)

William McKinley Osceola (Big Towns clan), a brother of Cory Osceola, became head man of Musa Isle, and later of Lasher's "Osceola Indian Village" attraction, which operated 1937–1943. As head of the village, the media dubbed William McKinley Osceola "chief." This is a "real photo" postcard from the 1930s. (95.77.1.)

Dr. John Harvey Kellogg, of cornflakes fame, operated the Battlecreek Sanitarium near Miami. He esteemed the health of the Seminoles, and made frequent and well publicized visits to examine the children at the Miami attractions. As seen in this postcard, Kellogg's visits produced some of the first "baby contests." Contemporary tribes continue to hold these contests at fairs today. (94.10.8.)

Seminoles parade on the infield at Hialeah Park Race Track on Derby Day, an annual event for decades, c. 1930s. (150g, photograph by Gleason Waite Romer; Courtesy of the Miami Dade-County Library System, Romer Collection.)

Alligator wrestler and Navy veteran of World War II, Moses Jumper (Panther clan) "puts the alligator to sleep" at the end of this 1950s performance at the *Jungle Queen* Seminole Village on New River in Ft. Lauderdale. Tips could net him $100 a day. Capt. Al Starts (in cap and tie on the left) was the creator of this attraction. (00.9.1, Betty Mae Jumper Collection.)

Young Seminole men, who first had to obtain permission from a member of the Snakeclan (a relative of the extinct Alligator clan) prior to wrestling alligators, sometimes traveled around the country performing the popular shows. Here Allan Jumper (Panther clan) wrestles at Animal Land in Lake George, New York in May 1959. (282–2, photograph by William D. Boehmer.)

"Forward to the Soil," held on January 29, 1927, was an audacious "land give-away ceremony" involving some 30 hired Seminoles. As the event was considered a potential threat to their sovereignty, the Seminole traditional council of elders was prompted to alert Washington and denounced Creek Seminole Tony Tommie (Panther clan) (in the war bonnet) for his active role in the event. (227, photograph by Claude C. Matlack.)

W. Stanley Hanson Sr. brought Seminoles from the Big Cypress to the 100th anniversary of the "Dade Massacre," which had initiated the lengthy Second Seminole War in December of 1835. At the event, the Seminoles invited Florida governor Sholtz to visit. He came to Tamiami Trail in February 1936. When Sholtz asked what he could do for them, the speakers frankly replied that they "wanted to be left alone." Pictured from left to right are as follows: Mike Osceola, unidentified, Stanley Hanson, Josie Billie, unidentified, Doctor Tiger, Jimmy Billie, Cory Osceola, and Gov. David Sholtz. (627, photograph by R.R. Doubleday.)

Seminole women produced a great volume of crafts for tourist sales. Here women at Silver Springs Seminole Village are engaged in morning activities, which would include fixing uniquely evolved hairstyles, smoothing long hair over a hair board, securing hairnets, and meticulously tying on layers of necklace beads for the day, c. 1940s. Shown here, from left to right, are Alice Doctor, Suzie Doctor, Ettie Cypress, Rosie Billie, Annie Tiger Tail, and Rachael Billie Boy. (1314.)

Jane Tiger Motlow (Otter clan) sews on a hand-cranked Singer sewing machine. The *i:laponi:* (Mikasuki) women excelled at patchwork, which became their signature art form. It was made by stripping fabric, sewing it together, then cutting and re-stitching the cloth in simple, straight bands to form intricate designs, *c.* 1927. (884.)

Alice Jim (Panther clan) sits on an Octagon soap-box in the work *chickee* to sew with her treadle Singer Sewing machine, *c.* 1925. As employment at tourist attractions and the commercialization of patchwork and other arts and crafts grew popular, women's artistic experimentation and production increased and the designs became more intricate. (50, photograph by Frank A. Robinson.)

Future Miccosukee Tribal Chairman, Buffalo Tiger (Bird clan), painted tourist souvenirs at Musa Isle Indian Village *c.* 1937. "Blue Bird" John Carillo, an Isleta from New Mexico, influenced the painting on drums as a winter employee at Musa Isle. (77, photograph by Florence I. Randle, WPA Photographer; Florence I. Randle Collection.)

A Kodachrome postcard shows members of the Tiger family (Bird clan) exhibiting a variety of arts and crafts in the 1940s. While the beaded belts appear to be imports, the patchwork clothing and palmetto fiber dolls were of native manufacture. (879, photograph by Charles C. Ebbets.)

71

Seminole men traditionally worked in wood. The canoe maker Charlie Cypress (Otter clan) also carved toy model canoes from cypress to sell to tourists, as seen here in a "real photo" postcard at the "Old Florida" camp in the Big Cypress, c. 1925. (97.1.18.)

Sam Willie (Bird clan) poses with a totem pole he carved, c. 1950. The poles, made with easily worked cypress, were first documented at Coppinger's around 1928. In 1938, Sam's brother Frank Willie made poles for the Musa Isle Village facade. They were a pan-Indian element that appealed to the Seminole craftsmen. (521, photograph by William D. Boehmer.)

Seven

MOVING OUT OF THE EVERGLADES TO THE TAMIAMI TRAIL

The Tamiami Trail was a road constructed between Miami and Naples, turning north along the west coast and terminating in Tampa. Cutting across Seminole canoe trails, it was opened to traffic in 1928. (95.2.9)

Many of the Seminoles in Miami attractions were from isolated Big Cypress and western Everglades camps. By the mid-1930s these people were ready to operate attractions of their own. Enterprising women such as Mokee Tiger and her daughter Effie Billie (Mrs. Ingraham) (Wind clan, both front center) approved of the new economic venture and moved their families "out to the road," meaning to the Tamiami Trail that ran through Collier County. (64, Washbon Family Collection.)

The Tamiami Trail camp of Jane Tiger Motlow (Otter clan) and her husband John Motlow (Bird clan) are pictured in a postcard, c. late 1930s. (94.15.3, photograph by R.R. Doubleday.)

John Osceola (Big Towns clan) poses outside his wife *Arteyee*'s large Bird clan camp in this postcard from the late 1930s. It became customary to fence the camps along the trail on the roadway with palmetto fans to provide privacy, crowd control, and an air of mystery. This camp had a bridge over the Tamiami Canal, the barrow pit from which the road was constructed. (1200, photograph by R.R. Doubleday.)

William McKinley Osceola (Big Towns clan, center) is shown at his wife's Bird clan camp in this postcard from the 1940s. With an income from tourism, family attractions on the Tamiami Trail allowed the participating Mikasuki-speakers to not only become totally self-sufficient, but to develop a strong sense of separatism and independence. (94.10.1, photograph by R.R. Doubleday.)

Chestnut Billie (Bird clan), who grew up in the Miami tourist attractions, was involved in the operation of this Bird clan camp where his mother Mona and father Charlie Billie (Wildcat clan) lived. This postcard is dated *c.* 1939. (1647, photograph by R.R. Doubleday.)

The Bird clan women at "Chestnut Billie's camp" included, from left to right, (front row) Maggie Billie Buster, Mona Billie, and Mona's unidentified sister; (back row) Pauline Tiger, Ruby Billie Clay, and Emma Tiger, *c.* 1939. (690, photograph by R.R. Doubleday).

This is the Otter clan camp of Camilla Tiger, third from left. Her husband John Poole Tiger (Bird clan) is second from left, *c.* 1940s. (1220, photograph by R.R. Doubleday.)

The Bear clan camp at Royal Palm Hammock was under the leadership of Billie Tommie Jumper, the matron in the back row (center), *c.* 1939. (579, photograph by R.R. Doubleday.)

Ruby Cypress (Panther clan) and Futch Cypress (Otter clan) were the elders in this Panther clan camp. Their daughter Juanita was married to Cory Osceola, who was the head-man at Musa Isle at an early age. Osceola was literate and very astute in the operation of a tourist attraction business, c. 1937. (99.4.1, photograph by R.R. Doubleday.)

In 1933, retired Episcopal deaconess Harriet M. Bedell came to south Florida from Alaska. A practical nurse, she saw that her new mission was to wean the Seminoles from the city tourist attractions and create a viable crafts market for their off-season wares. At Glade Cross Mission in Everglade City, Bedell was close to the Tamiami Trail and Big Cypress camps. (88.2.27.)

Bedell was finally tolerated, if not accepted, in Seminole camps. Here, she is poled in a canoe by one of the most traditional practitioners of the native religion, the bundle-carrier Ingraham Billie (Panther clan). (88.2.37.)

Bedell poses with *Aklophi*, Mrs. Billie (Panther clan), the oldest Seminole woman in 1935. An accomplished medical practitioner, she was also known to children on the trail as *Mach Hamochie*, "Old Lady." Annie (Panther clan) and Frank Charlie (Wind clan) were Bedell's frequent companions. Frank drove her car and sometimes served as a photographer. (93.11.10.)

Bedell involved herself in the crafts market and enforced some strong artistic restrictions, which over time made the crafts produced for Glade Cross Mission (especially patchwork) atypical. Billie Tommie Jumper and her daughter Ruby Cypress (Bear clan, with Billy and Sally) made novel "waste" and "market" baskets for Bedell, using traditional Seminole materials and weaving techniques. (93.11.8.)

Eight

RESERVATIONS FOR SOME, BUSINESS AS USUAL FOR OTHERS

As a whole, the Florida Seminoles shunned the government. Having little luck enticing the Seminoles onto a reservation in the Big Cypress, the Seminole Agency moved operations to Dania (shown here in 1938), near Ft. Lauderdale, in 1925. (456, photograph by William D. Boehmer.)

Ivy C. Stranahan, wife of the former trading post operator and avid activist for Seminole welfare, persuaded the first family to move to the reservation, originally deemed for "sick and indigent Indians." Creek Seminole Annie Jumper Tommie (Panther clan) became the matriarch of the new reservation community after being moved from Ft. Lauderdale under threat of displacement by the City Fathers. (190, photograph by Frank A. Robinson.)

Traditional government continued to prevail over the Seminoles, with laws of conduct enforced by their council of elders, the holders and owners of powerful medicine bundles. Shown in a "real photo" postcard, from left to right, are Elders Tom "Homespun" Billie (Otter clan), John Willie (Bird clan), and bundle-carrier Billy Motlow (Panther clan). (485.)

Creek Seminole missionaries arrived in Florida from Oklahoma around 1907. They arrived at the northern camps of the Creek Seminoles, hoping that their Florida brethren would learn to follow the "Jesus Road." Though rebuffed, their persistence paid off when conversions finally came from this Snake clan family in 1920. Pictured here from left to right are children Lena and Pocahontas Huff (both Panther clan), Annie Mae Tommie, and baby Frank Huff (panther clan), Mary Tustenuggee Tiger (Snake clan), Tudie Tommie, Ada Tiger (snake clan) 3 unidentified men, Jack Tommie (Panther clan), Sam tommie (Panther clan), and two unidentified men.

Everglade Cross Mission was operated by the Episcopalian Church in the Big Cypress. Though well-meaning, it was a fruitless and short-lived project that attempted to bring Christianity and medical services to the Seminoles. The commissary is shown in 1915. (92.19.4, James W. Covington Collection.)

John Collier, the Commissioner of Indian Affairs and author of the Indians' New Deal (a reformation of the previous Dawes Act, which embraced the concept of Indian termination and acculturation) emphasized the preservation of native culture and folkways. Desiring to see a pristine Seminole camp, Collier was taken to Lillian Stone Buster's (Wildcat clan) camp in the Big Cypress at Deep Lake in 1935. Seen here, from left to right, are Charlie Billie Boy, John Collier, Annie Billie Boy, and Rachael Billie Boy. (91.5P.25, William D. and Edith M. Boehmer Collection.)

The next day a formal meeting was held at West Palm Beach with Collier and Secretary of the Interior Harold Ickes. The group of Creek Seminoles, under the leadership of Sam Tommie (Panther clan), petitioned the government for a reservation in their area. This meeting was met with the near-violent disapproval of the traditional council and spokesmen. The reservation and concessions, however, were granted. (24, photograph by Ray Dame.)

As part of Collier's New Deal to the Seminoles, the Creeks received emaciated cattle from the Dust Bowl states. Surviving cattle became the nucleus for the very successful Seminole cattle enterprise. Here cowboys brand cattle on the Brighton Reservation, *c.* 1940s. (5-8035-34, Courtesy of Fort Lauderdale Historical Society.)

All of the cattle initially received the U.S. brand, but over time cattle were purchased by individuals who gave them their own personal brand. Brighton cattlemen, from left to right, are Willie Gopher, Joe Henry Tiger, Jack Smith, Frank Huff, Andrew Jackson Bowers, John Josh, Naha Tiger, Toby Johns, Frank Shore, John Henry Gopher, Lonnie Buck, Charlie Micco, and Harjo Osceola, *c.* 1950. (472–8, photograph by William D. Boehmer.)

Big Cypress later received a herd. Shown here are Frank Billie, Frank J. Billie, Morgan Smith (a Creek Seminole overseer), Willie Frank, Josie Billie, Jimmy Cypress, Charlie Osceola, Junior Cypress, Johnny Cypress, and Little Fewell. (91.5P.26, photograph by Joseph Janney Steinmetz; William D. and Edith M. Boehmer Collection.)

Dipping cattle against ticks that caused "deer tick fever" was compulsory in Florida. Deer were the supposed carriers of the disease, and a controversy arose over killing off the supposed animals. Off-reservation Seminoles requested Ickes's involvement, and due to his request for more studies, the Seminoles' deer were saved, c. 1940. (13–3, photograph by William D. Boehmer.)

Willie Gopher Sr. (Panther clan) and Fred Montesdeoca, an agricultural extension agent, remove screw worms from the ears of a calf and provide treatment during an epidemic. Montesdeoca came to work for the Bureau of Indian Affairs in 1938 and retired in 1971. (94.88.13.)

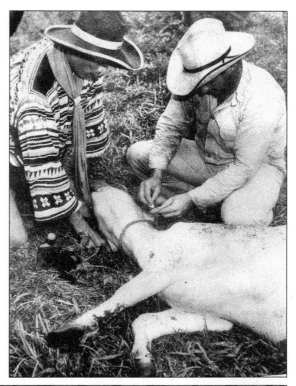

A school was one of the requested concessions of the Creek Seminole petitioners. This postcard shows teacher William D. Boehmer and his wife Edith, a much-loved Indian Service couple who came to the isolated Brighton Reservation in 1938. The Boehmers would coordinate Seminole tribal education until their retirement in 1965, and William Boehmer also left a legacy of photographs that he made. (00.52.1.)

Edith Boehmer's job title was "housekeeper," a requisite vocation for the wives of Indian Service schoolteachers. However, she was soon asked to sell a few of the Seminole women's palmetto fiber dolls. Edith organized the women and the men carvers to form a very successful craft guild. Here, Annie Tiger (Mrs. Richard Osceola, Panther clan) poses with one of her dolls, *c.* 1939. (91.5P.31, photograph by William D. Boehmer.)

An unidentified Civilian Conservation Corps–Indian Division worker runs telephone line on the Brighton Reservation, c. 1938. The Florida Seminoles benefited much from the CCC-ID, mainly from roads and improved pasturage that upgraded the reservations. (75–N–SEM–C–891333, Courtesy of National Archives.)

W. Stanley Hanson, co-founder of the Seminole Indian Association, was hired to initiate the CCC-ID program on the Big Cypress Reservation in 1937; at that time, there were only 14 residents. Hanson's lifetime relationship with the Big Cypress Seminoles brought his friend, the influential leader Josie Billie, to the reservation. Billie influenced his followers and by 1938 there were 90 residents. (1013, photograph by Ray K. Williams.)

On the Hollywood Reservation, Betty Mae Tiger (Snake clan) wanted to learn to read, but no area schools—white or black—would take her. Betty, her cousin Agnes, and brother Howard were eventually sent to Cherokee Indian School in Cherokee, North Carolina, and other students soon followed. Pictured are George Huff Storm (Panther clan), Howard Tiger (Snake clan), Agnes Parker (Snake clan), Betty Tiger, and Moses Jumper (Panther clan), in 1939. (9–21, photograph by William D. Boehmer.)

In July of 1940, the noted ethnomusicologist Frances Densmore came to Florida to collect songs from the Seminoles for the Library of Congress. These Creek Seminole men are recording at the Brighton Reservation. From left to right, unidentified, Robert Osceola, Billy Bowlegs, Naha Tiger, and John Josh sing songs for Densmore's wire recording. (9–11, photograph by William D. Boehmer.)

At the end of Roundup there was a Field Day celebration with contests. Here a tug-of-war is underway at a Big Cypress Field Day in the early 1940s. (536–5–28, photograph by William D. Boehmer.)

As World War II loomed on the horizon, the Florida Seminoles refused to sign registration forms for the draft (due to old post-war edicts against signing papers), but leaders said they would be glad to fight. Aware of their "Unconquered" status, the newspapers applauded them for stepping into the production line and "Doing Their Part to Win the War." This included picking crops when other farm workers were drafted or enlisted, May 1942. (687.)

Due to educational requirements, few Florida Seminoles were eligible for military service. One exception was 18-year-old Howard Tiger (Snake clan), who eagerly enlisted in the Marine Corps on August 18, 1943. He and his schoolmate Moses Jumper (Navy, Panther clan) saw plenty of action in the Pacific theater of war. (5–8428, Courtesy of Ft. Lauderdale Historical Society.)

During the fall of 1948, hurricanes and heavy rainfall created high water levels. Since 95 percent of the 36,000-acre reservation was under water, 85 Seminoles from Brighton Reservation had to be evacuated to higher ground. The Red Cross furnished them with aid and moved families into army tents that were pitched on a palmetto prairie near Popash Slough, west of Okeechobee, Florida. (448–2, photograph by William D. Boehmer.)

Seminole cattle at Brighton also had a rough time in the fall of 1948. Here they seek the spoil banks from drainage ditches—the only high ground available in their pasture. (487–18, Photograph by William D. Boehmer.)

Lee Billie Cypress (Panther clan) greets census takers at her Big Cypress camp *Ahfachkee* in 1950. (91.5P.27, photograph by *Miami Herald* staff; William D. and Edith M. Boehmer Collection.)

Down on the Tamiami Trail in the late 1940s, the airplane propeller–powered air-boat was a new vehicle at camps. Excellent for gigging frogs (a lucrative, but short-lived, economy), air-boats were later used to transport tourists to the Everglades. (402, photograph by Annette Rada; Courtesy of the Historical Museum, Miami.)

The acculturated Seminole Larry Mike Osceola (Bird clan), who had grown up at Musa Isle attraction, ran a thriving tourist attraction business on the trail during the 1950s. (83–125–240, Courtesy of Florida State Archives.)

A Creek Baptist from Oklahoma, the Rev. Willie King came to Florida with his wife Lena and daughter Ruth in the 1930s. He became pastor of the new First Seminole Indian Baptist Church in 1937, the first church allowed on the reservations, at Dania, Florida. Reverend King taught himself the Mikasuki language so that he could better serve his congregation. (97.27.6, Courtesy of P.K. Yonge Library of Florida History.)

This is a photograph of the First Seminole Baptist Church on the Dania Reservation. The sign is in Creek. While it was being built in 1937, the traditional people from the trail used to circle this building and blow smoke to make bad medicine. Pictured are Minnie Bert and Pauline Bert (Panther clan), c. 1948. (399, photograph by Annette Rada; Courtesy of the Historical Museum, Miami.)

95

Rev. Stanley Smith, an Oklahoma Creek, arrived in 1943 and made unprecedented conversions. One included the traditional religious leader Josie Billie (Panther clan), who in turn persuaded 21 of his followers to follow suit. The Big Cypress Baptist Church (seen here) opened in 1948. Josie Billie was the assistant pastor and was licensed to preach by the Southern Baptists in 1949 at the age of 60. (91.5P.28, photograph by William D. Boehmer.)

Ingraham Billie (Panther clan) was given the medicine bundle that his brother Josie Billie had held in trust when he accepted Christianity. Much later, Ingraham Billie also moved to the Big Cypress and became a Christian, but he retained his bundle and continued to conduct Corn Dances. (98.27.14, Louis Capron Collection; Courtesy of P.K. Yonge Library of Florida History, Gainesville.)

As Southern Baptists, Rev. and Mrs. Genus Crenshaw saw a lengthy and fulfilling mission to the Seminoles. They pose here with Seminole lay preachers in the 1950s. From left to right are Frank Charlie (Wind clan), Junior Billie (Panther clan), and Creek Seminole Jack Micco. (98.31.12, Courtesy of the Home Mission Board.)

When the traditional people would not allow the few resident Christians to build a Baptist Church on the Brighton reservation, the Lykes Brothers Corporation donated a small plot adjacent to the reservation for a church. This congregation met there on Christmas Day 1956. (83–025–260, Courtesy of Florida State Archives.)

Creek Seminole Frank Shore (Panther clan), a prominent stockman and cattleman, was the bundle-carrier for the Creek Seminoles beginning in the 1950s. He officiated at the Creeks' Green Corn Dance held at Hilola. Here he is seen in traditional clothes, November 7, 1960. (444–3, photograph by William D. Boehmer.)

Nine

THE THREAT OF TERMINATION CREATES TWO TRIBES

The termination of Indian tribes was a federal cutback following World War II. However, since the Florida Seminoles had many supporters who realized that they were not ready to face termination, the Seminoles were allowed to form a federally recognized tribe. Here Creek Seminole Billy Osceola (on the microphone) explains plans leading to the adoption of a tribal charter and constitution, *c.* 1954. (487–24, photograph by William D. Boehmer.)

Members of the constitution and charter committee pose together in March of 1957. Pictured from left to right are Rex Quinn, L. Mike Osceola (Bird clan), Frank Billie (Wind clan), Jackie Willie, Bill Osceola (Bird clan), Creek Seminole John Henry Gopher (Bird clan), Creek Seminole Billy Osceola (Bird clan), and Jimmie O. Osceola (Panther clan.) (184–3, photograph by William D. Boehmer.)

Democratic voting by ballot was a new practice for Florida Seminoles, as was electing leaders that were not necessarily from the traditional leadership clan, the Panther clan. Shown here in August of 1957, Louise Billie (Otter clan) and Sam Huff (Big Towns clan) vote to accept the constitution and bylaws in order to create the newest federally recognized tribe, the Seminole Tribe of Florida. (91.5P.32, William D. and Edith M. Boehmer collection.)

Seminole family income was very low. The "Friends of the Seminoles" organization, based in Ft. Lauderdale, bought clothing for Seminole students before they began the new school year. Mrs. Moen, a member of the "Friends," had a store in Dania where these students are selecting clothing, c. 1956. (260–1, photograph by William D. Boehmer.)

Jane Motlow (Otter clan) waits for Connie Frank (Otter clan) to board the Greyhound Bus that will take her to school at the Haskell Institute in Lawrence, Kansas, September 1956. (236–2, photograph by William D. Boehmer.)

Members of the Tribal Council of the Seminole Tribe of Florida are pictured from left to right in 1959: Frank Billie (Wind clan), Mike Osceola (Bird clan), John Cypress (Panther clan), John Josh (Deer clan), Billie Osceola (Chairman, Bird clan), Laura Mae Jumper Osceola (Secretary, Panther clan), Betty Mae Tiger Jumper (Snake clan), Charlotte Tommie Osceola (Snake clan), and Howard Tiger (Snake clan). (464, photograph by William D. Boehmer.)

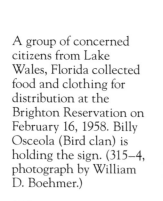

A group of concerned citizens from Lake Wales, Florida collected food and clothing for distribution at the Brighton Reservation on February 16, 1958. Billy Osceola (Bird clan) is holding the sign. (315–4, photograph by William D. Boehmer.)

Seminoles' income in the latter 1950s was derived largely from tourist craft markets, alligator wrestling, crop picking, parking lot attention, cattle farming, or preaching. A new economy emerged around 1954 and consisted of cutting newly unfolding palm sprays, demonstrated here by Creek Seminole Arlene Johns (Panther clan). The sprays would be sold to contractors would who in turn market them to churches for Palm Sunday. (172–1, photograph by William D. Boehmer.)

Thanks to constant efforts by the Friends of the Seminoles, Seminole school children were accepted into local schools by the late 1940s. However, many students still lived in camp *chickees* with no source of lighting or plumbing; just a pump, primitive shower, and latrine by a tree. This formulated the Friends' next mission. (535–0–4, photograph by William D. Boehmer.)

Since many small wooden tourist cottages were being replaced by modern motels or homes, the Friends attempted to locate donors and move these structures to the reservation. By floating loans for the Seminole homeowners to electrify and plumb, the Friends helped the Seminole Indian Estates subdivision on the Hollywood reservation to take shape. Here David and Eugene Bowers (Snake clan) play outside their new home in 1956. (02.7.1.)

As the new homes were furnished with electric stoves and refrigerators, workshops for their use were conducted by the local power-company. A home demonstration agent was also called in, and in 1956, a housekeeping contest was held with prizes donated by the Salvation Army. Mrs. Barnes (judge), Mary Bowers (first place, Snake clan), Martha Osceola (second place, Panther clan), Betty Mae Jumper (third place, Snake clan), and Ivy C. Stranahan (founder, Friends of the Seminoles) are pictured here. (24121, Courtesy of the Florida State Archives.)

The Rev. Bill Osceola (Bird clan) built his own concrete block home, posing here around 1960. (518–33, photograph by William D. Boehmer.)

With help from area merchants and associations, the Seminole tribe sponsored their first rodeo in order to raise funds to send representatives to the capitols at Tallahassee and Washington, D.C to oversee tribal affairs. The proceeds of future rodeos also went towards loans from organizations such as the Friends. (268–1, photograph by William D. Boehmer.)

One of the features of the rodeos was a princess contest. These young women were the contestants on September 5, 1960. Shown, from left to right, are Lola Gopher, Gladys Bowers, Nancy Osceola, Ruby Nelson, Elsie Johns, Lawanna Osceola, Connie Johns, Dorothy Tommie, Priscilla Doctor, and Judybill Osceola. (324–7, photograph by William D. Boehmer.)

November 11, 1959 was the formal opening date of Seminole Indian Estates on the Hollywood Reservation. Pictured, from left to right, are the following: William D. Boehmer (Seminole Education), Creek Seminole Billy Osceola (Bird clan, Chairman of the Tribal Council), Mrs. Hugh Hale (Representative of the Florida Woman's Club), Indian Commissioner Glenn Emmons, Virgil N. Harrington (Superintendent of the Seminole Agency), and Bill Osceola (Bird clan, President of the Seminole Tribe of Florida, Inc.'s Board of Directors). (171–1, photograph by William D. Boehmer.)

At the Seminole Indian Estates dedication ceremonies, from left to right, are Charlotte Tommie Osceola (Snake clan), Betty Mae Jumper (Snake clan), Dorothy Osceola (Panther clan), Ivy C. Stranahan, Mrs. Hugh Hale, unidentified, and Mrs. F. D. Sheldon. The club women were representatives of the Friends of the Seminoles, the local Daughters of the American Revolution, and the Florida Women's Club, all major supporters of the Seminoles. (520–2, photograph by William D. Boehmer.)

The 1960s saw numerous Seminole high school graduates. Here Priscilla Doctor (Snake clan) and Judy Bill Osceola (Otter clan), graduates of McArthur Senior High School, are pictured on prom night, June 3, 1960. (322–1, photograph by William D. Boehmer.)

In 1962 Joe Dan (Jaudon) Osceola (Panther clan), who was the first Florida Seminole to graduate from a Florida public high school, was attending Georgetown University in Kentucky. He was aided by scholarships from the Florida Federation of Women's Clubs and the Circus of Saints and Sinners Seminole Indian Foundation, Inc. (91.5P.33, William D. and Edith M. Boehmer Collection.)

The Seminole Arts and Crafts Guild, begun at Brighton, continued to produce quality Seminole-made goods for sale with participation from the Big Cypress and Hollywood reservations. Creek Seminole Agnes Johns (Bird clan) poses with an array of patchwork skirts, c. 1955. (443–7, photograph by William D. Boehmer.)

Following termination proceedings for the Florida Seminoles in 1954, the non-reservation "Seminoles," (future members of the Miccosukee Tribe) had to alert the federal government about the two separate groups of people whom the government was labeling "Florida Seminoles." On scant funds, and without adequate clothing for northern weather, representatives traveled to Washington, D.C. Shown from left to right are Jimmie Billie (Wind clan), George Osceola (Deer clan), and Buffalo Tiger (Bird clan). (94.118.1.)

Not interested in joining with the Seminoles, the Trail Indians sought separate recognition. In those volatile times, they received Washington's attention and the front-page coverage they needed with a trip to Communist Cuba in July 1959. In Havana, from left to right, were (front row) John Willie, John M. Osceola, Raymond Tiger Tail, two unidentified people, Buffalo Tiger, and Howard M. Osceola; and (back row) Stanley Frank, Homer Osceola, and Billy M. Osceola. (157, photograph by Mike Freeman; Jane Wood Reno Collection.)

This was a meeting with Commissioner of Indian Affairs at the Miccosukees' headquarters, the *Chickeechobee*. The large *chickee* represented the tribal seat of government that was federally recognized in 1962 as the Miccosukee Tribe of Indians of Florida. At the table from left to right, are Leo Alpert, tribal attorney Morton Silver, Morrill Tozier, Commissioner Glenn Emmons, and spokesman and future Miccosukee Chairman Buffalo Tiger (Bird clan), December 1954. (333, Jane Wood Reno Collection.)

Both tribes received substantial educational improvements and economic support from the Bureau of Indian Affairs. This is the "Seminole Okalee Indian Village & Crafts Center" on the Hollywood Seminole (formerly Dania) reservation, shown in a postcard c. 1960s. (02.5.1, photograph by J.F. Capicotto.)

The BIA built a restaurant for the Miccosukee Tribe to operate on the Tamiami Trail near Jimmie Tiger's popular Indian Village attraction, postcard c. 1960s. (94.10.13, photograph by Bill Levy.)

Like the Seminole tribe, the Miccosukees received a school. They created more traditional, bilingual programs for their students. In this visiting group is Ivy C. Stranahan of the Friends of the Seminoles with the longtime Miccosukee Tribal Chairman Buffalo Tiger (Bird clan.) (The others are not identified). (518–30, photograph by William D. Boehmer.)

The first tribal member to graduate from a local high school, Joe Dan Osceola (Panther clan), became president of the board of directors. Betty Mae Tiger Jumper (Snake clan), the first Seminole to seek a formal education, was elected as chairman or "chief" of the Seminole Council. Pictured in this postcard c. 1968, she is the only woman who has held that position in the Seminole tribe (1967–1971). (977.)

Frank Willie (Bird clan) gave his old tourist attraction camp to his nephew, Jimmie Tiger (Bird clan), seen here. In the 1960s it became a well-known attraction with air-boat rides. In the 1970s, Jimmie Tiger offered his business to the Miccosukee Tribe, which operates the high-profile attraction to promote the tribe's cultural activities. This postcard is dated c. 1960s. (95.80.1.)

Ten

PROSPERITY WAS JUST AROUND THE CORNER

Jacob Osceola, SPEC 4, Army (Panther clan) stands on a runway during the Vietnam War in the 1960s. Many Florida Seminoles entered the service during that time and came home with new skills that enabled them to manage tribal departments and to assume major political positions in the tribe. (93.80.1. Eloise Osceola Collection.)

Robert Osceola (Bird clan) leads a group of children enrolled in the Seminole tribe's Head Start Program in a social dance of the Green Corn Dance. (78.1.1, photograph by Patsy West.)

While "Smoke Shops" for tax-free tobacco products was the Seminoles' first economic boon, bingo and gaming ventures proved to be even more successful and were introduced to other tribes by the Florida Indians. This August 1984 photograph shows Seminole Bingo on the Tampa Reservation, Coontaunchobee, near Bobby Henry's Seminole Indian Village. (91.5P.34, photograph by William D. Boehmer.)

Tina Marie Osceola, granddaughter of Cory R. Osceola, represented the Seminole Tribe of Florida as Junior Miss and then Miss Seminole in 1984. A championship fancy shawl dancer, Tina accompanied her family to pow wows throughout the country. (93.34.32, photograph by Bill Held, Tina M. Osceola Collection.)

Seminole chairman James E. Billie (Bird clan) escorts Florida pioneer environmentalist Marjorie Stoneman Douglas, who in her youth penned *Everglades River of Grass*, to the festival at Smallwood's Trading Post. (95.13.1, photo by Peter Gallagher.)

Elicia Sanchez (Panther clan) and Geraldine Osceola (Panther clan) pose in Betty Mae Jumper's booth of Seminole crafts at the 1991 Red Earth Pow Wow in Oklahoma City, Oklahoma. (91.6.1, photograph by Patsy West.)

Independent Seminole Bobby Henry (left) and Alan Jumper (Panther clan) (right) wait to be judged in a clothing-contest at Trading Post Days at Smallwood's Trading Post, Chokoloskee, Florida, March 1992. (92.16.13, photograph by Patsy West.)

Medicine/religious leader Pete Osceola Sr.'s (Panther clan) "Gator Hut" was a popular booth at the annual Seminole Fair. (92.13. 25, photograph by Patsy West.)

Seminoles participate in the reenactment of the Dade Battle. Here, Billy L. Cypress (Bear clan), executive director of the tribe's Ah-Tah-Thi-Ki Museum, assumes the role of Chief Jumper and relates the Seminoles' strategy to the watching audience at the Bushnell, Florida battleground. (95.1.4, photograph by Patsy West.)

As the eldest woman in the Seminole Tribe, Suzie Billie (Panther clan) has shared her vast knowledge of herbal medicine and cultural mores with tribal members and the media. (02.8.1, photograph by Janet Finnegan; Courtesy of the Creative Source.)

Most Seminole women elders wear their patchwork clothing daily. Tommie Jumper (Panther clan), Ruby Cypress (Bear clan), and Betty Mae Jumper (Snake clan) put on their best to compete for prize money at the Seminole Fair on the Hollywood Reservation. (93.17.18, photograph by Patsy West.)

The Seminole Color Guard participates in events around the country. Here veterans of Vietnam Paul Bowers (Panther clan, Big Cypress Representative), Mitchell Cypress (Otter clan, President of the Seminole Tribe of Florida and the present acting chairman), and Steven Bowers (Deer clan, Governor's Council in Indian Affairs Representative) pose in Orlando, Florida. (93.17.2, photograph by Patsy West.)

Buffalo Tiger (Bird clan), the founding chairman of the Miccosukee Tribe of Indians of Florida and present owner of "Buffalo Tiger's Florida Everglades Air-boat Rides," pauses to tell his guests about the Everglades ecosystem, which is quite important to the Miccosukee tribal members who live along the Tamiami Trail. (93.56.5, photograph by Patsy West.)

The Independent Seminoles do not belong to either federally recognized tribe. Independent Seminole leader Bobby Clay (Bird clan) and Ruby Clay (Big Towns clan) sell crafts at a fair. (94.78.19, photograph by Jimmie O. Osceola [Panther clan].)

Noted photographer John Gillan created a collection of photographs centering around Smallwood's Store, a historic site, where Chief Charlie and Winter Dawn Osceola posed for this portrait in 1996. (02.13.1, Courtesy of John Gillan.)

Melissa Osceola, a future Seminole tribal princess, poses in her jingle dress at the Seminole Tribe's large pow wow, "Discover Native America," held in 1994 at Jacksonville, Florida. The event attracted champion Native American dancers who competed for large cash prizes. (94.30.16, photograph by Patsy West.)

This sign serves as a historical reminder of Jack Tiger Tail (see page 58) as it gestures towards the entrance of the Seminole tribe's Big Cypress tourist attraction, "Billie Swamp Safari." The attraction was named for Kissimmee Billie (Wind clan), whose Panther wife *Aklophi* had a nearby camp. (96.28.1, photograph by Patsy West.)

Billie Swamp Safari features exotic animals in a natural habitat, such as this herd of water buffalo. Visitors see the attraction on a "Swamp Buggy." Interestingly enough, the endangered Florida panthers that share this habitat are feeding on the fast breeding exotics, which ultimately may aide in maintaining their population. (97.26.8, photograph by Patsy West.)

The Seminole Tribal Headquarters is located on the Hollywood Reservation. Seminole tribal member Robert Kippenberger (Panther clan) is a professional photographer. (02.10.1, Courtesy of Robert Kippenberger.)

James E. Billie, an accomplished pilot and chairman of the Seminole Tribe of Florida (shown here during his fourth term in 1997), disembarks from a helicopter he has just flown from his home on the Big Cypress reservation. The helio-pad is on the roof of the Seminole Tribal Headquarters Building. (97.26.2, photograph by Patsy West.)

A still photograph taken during the filming of the Seminole tribe's Ah-Tah-Thi-Ki Museum's five-screen introductory film *We Seminoles*, made in 1997, shows Ronnie B. and Elmira Billie and their children with Henry John Billie (Wind clan) poling the canoe. (97.26.1, photograph by Patsy West.)

Betty Mae Tiger Jumper (Snake clan) was awarded a Doctorate of Humane Letters by Florida State University in 1994. An avid story teller, she holds her book *Legends of the Seminoles* in 1995. The book is based on folk tales that her grandmother Mary Tustenuggee Tiger (Snake clan) told her and is illustrated by Guy La Bree. (97.20.3, photograph by Peter Gallagher; Betty Mae Jumper Collection.)

Ah-Tah-Thi-Ki Museum, "A Place to Learn, A Place to Remember," opened on the Big Cypress Reservation on August 21, 1997. Pictured here from left to right are Carla Cypress (Panther clan), Sally Buster (Bear clan), and William Cypress (Panther clan). (02.9.1, photograph by Tom Gallaher; Courtesy of Tom Gallaher.)

A third-generation alligator wrestler, Thomas Storm (Otter clan) carries an alligator to the wrestling pit for his show at the 1998 reopening of Okalee Museum and Village, Hollywood Reservation. (98.34.1, photograph by Patsy West.)

With about 650 members, the Miccosukee Tribe of Indians of Florida greatly benefits from their Miccosukee Resort and Gaming complex, located near the Tamiami Trail. It opened on July 14, 1999. (02.12.1, photograph by Ernie Tiger; Courtesy of Seminole Communications, Seminole Tribe of Florida.)

Posing after a roundup on the Big Cypress Seminole reservation, from left to right, are Rudy Osceola (Panther clan), Paul Bowers (Panther clan), Michael Henry (Panther clan), Joey Henry (Panther clan), and Ayze Tommie (Bird clan). The Seminole tribe is the 19th-largest producer of calves in the nation. (02.10.3, photograph by Robert Kippenberger [Panther clan]; Courtesy of Robert Kippenberger.)

The Seminole tribe is very active in the rodeo arena. The tribe hosts national competitions, and tribal members travel to and participate in other Indian Rodeo events around the country. (02.12.2, Courtesy of Seminole Communications, Seminole Tribe of Florida.)

Sonny Billie (Panther clan), former chairman of the Miccosukee Tribe of Indians of Florida, was the leading bundle-carrier for the tribal people. He performed social dances at Ah-Tah-Thi-Ki Museum's Living Village in 1999. (99.30.1, photograph by Patsy West.)

This was the Seminole Tribe's original Coconut Creek Casino. Other gaming facilities are at Brighton, Immokalee, Ft. Pierce, Big Cypress, and at their Hard Rock Hotels and Casinos at Hollywood and Tampa, Florida. (02.10.2, photograph by Robert Kippenberger.)

A conceptual drawing of the Hollywood Seminole Hard Rock Hotel and Casino, Hollywood Reservation that opened in 2004. In December 6, 2006 the Seminole Tribe purchased Hard Rock International's 124 Hard Rock Cafes, hotels and casinos across the world. (02.10.2, Courtesy of Seminole Communications, Seminole Tribe of Florida.)

The Seminole Rodeo Princess brings in the flag at the Big Cypress reservation's Junior Cypress Rodeo Arena. (02.12.4, Courtesy of Seminole Communications, Seminole Tribe of Florida.)

Lightning Source UK Ltd.
Milton Keynes UK
UKHW050453021221
394807UK00001B/22